TIMEWARP

Greece
anthology

TABLE OF CONTENTS

I Am Ancient Greece	1
In the Names of Gods and Goddesses	2
The Way It Was	3
Were the Greeks Just Horsing Around?	5
Power in Ancient Greece	13
Living and Learning in Ancient Greece	20
The Birth of Democracy	25
Feathers and Foul Play	32
Ye Gods!	38
Magnificent Apollo	46
May the Best Weaver Win	47
Hera and the Two Bears	52
Let the Plays Begin!	58
On Beetle's Wings	62
The Beauty of It All	72
Great Greeks	77
Aesop's Fables: Lessons for Life	78

I Am Ancient Greece

I am ancient Greece,
Land of the thundering gods.
I am the seed from which modern civilization sprouted,
A beautiful country of mountains and islands,
Caressed by three magnificent seas.
Within my boundaries, democracy was born,
As were the spirited games of champions.
Withstanding the winds of time,
I am Sparta, Athens, Delphi, and Crete.
I am thoughtful, proud, strong, resourceful.
I am ancient Greece.

In the Names of Gods and Goddesses

My name is Gaea.
My name is Gaea.
The god of the sky made me his wife.
I gave all the plants and animals life.
My name is Gaea.
My name is Gaea.

My name is Zeus.
My name is Zeus.
I put the sun and the moon up in the sky.
I can change the weather with the blink of an eye.
My name is Zeus.
My name is Zeus.

My name is Hera.
My name is Hera.
My wedding was so joyous it lasted 300 years,
But my marriage was disastrous and filled with tears.
My name is Hera.
My name is Hera.

My name is Ares.
My name is Ares.
I stir up trouble with all my might.
I say the bigger the battle, the better the fight.
My name is Ares.
My name is Ares.

My name is Hermes.
My name is Hermes.
I serve as messenger to my father, Zeus.
I can move like the wind with wings on my shoes.
My name is Hermes.
My name is Hermes.

THE WAY IT WAS

Greece began long ago. At first, it was a small group of islands. The people lived in caves. They gathered food. They hunted. Time passed. They hunted more and fished.

Some moved to the mainland. Villages formed. Villagers made pottery and tools. They began to trade things for food.

The most successful people in this early time lived on Crete. It was the largest Greek island. The people were called the Minoans. They lived well in 2000 B.C.

A second group took over the island about 1600 B.C. They were the Mycenae. They came from the mainland. The Minoans died out after they came. It was around 1400 B.C. No one knows why they died. Parts of their villages were found in the 1920s. They showed what the people cared about, such as trade and art.

The Mycenae were in power until 1100 B.C. A great war was fought in their time. It was the Trojan War. The Greeks fought the men of Troy. Troy was a city near Greece. The armies fought because a Greek woman was kidnapped.

Life in Greece faded after the war. Things turned around in 800 B.C. The number of people grew. The Greeks got in touch with the rest of the world again. Other changes took place. The country began a "Golden Age" in 500 B.C. Athens was the strongest city. It was richest, too. This age ended when another group took over. They were the Macedonians. Alexander the Great led them. He began to rule Greece in 336 B.C.

Alexander the Great died in 323 B.C. The Greek lands were split. They were shared among his officers. They fought each other. The fights weakened the country. Romans attacked. Rome took over Greece by 30 B.C.

Were the Greeks Just Horsing Around?

Around 700 B.C., a great poet began to write stories he had heard about a great war. It was the Trojan War. There were many stories about it. The Greek people liked hearing them because it was a war they had won. Homer wrote a long poem about it. The poem was called The Iliad.

About 2,000 years later, a German man read the poem. He believed the story it told was true. Other people did not. The man decided to prove it was true. He went in search of the city that once was called Troy. It was where the war had been fought. He found the city. He also found the bones of people and animals. He found the remains of buildings, too. He found a lot of other things. Many people believe he found proof that Homer's story of war was true.

The kingdom of Troy stood almost 3,000 years ago. The place where it stood now is called Turkey. It was a great walled kingdom. The stone wall had been built to protect the people of the city. It was a strong wall. In some places, it was very tall. The bottom was very slippery. It was hard for enemies to get past the wall.

The only way into the city was through a large wooden gate. People passed in and out with goods to sell or trade. Men stood guard over the gate at night. It was the key to the safety of the city.

The king of Troy was named Priam. He ruled over much of the surrounding land and the sea. He was very powerful, but he wanted more. He wanted to be greater than his enemies, the Greeks.

The land in Greece was not good for growing some crops. The Greek people had to sail across the sea to buy some things they needed. To get where they wanted to go, they had to pass Troy. When they did, King Priam made them pay.

The Greek ships were not warships. They were not fast. They could not outrun the Trojans. So, the Greek sailors had to pay the toll. They paid with gold, oil, and other goods.

The Greeks did not like paying to use the sea. They threatened war with Troy if King Priam did not stop his unfair ways. King Priam did not worry about the Greek threats. The wall would protect his kingdom.

Time passed, and the Trojans continued to stop Greek ships as they tried to sail past Troy. But, they did something else that was much worse. It would lead to their downfall. Stop

Sparta was a city-state in Greece. Its king was named Menelaus. He was married to the most beautiful woman in the world. Her name was Helen. The Trojans kidnapped her! They carried her away to marry Paris, the prince of Troy.

Menelaus vowed to rescue Helen. Sparta was known to have some of the greatest fighters in the world. But, they would be no match for the Trojans and their friends. The Spartans needed help.

Menelaus sent word to his brother. King Agamemnon ruled over another Greek state. He prayed before a statue of the goddess Athena. He offered a bull as a gift. He asked for victory over the Trojans. Menelaus also sent word to the state of Ithaca. Prince Odysseus of Ithaca agreed to fight with the brothers. Greek ships set sail for Troy.

King Priam soon learned that the Greeks were headed for Troy. He was not worried. Still, he went to pray to Athena. He, too, asked for victory. He offered a ram as a gift.

The Greeks landed on the shores of Troy. The Trojans opened the gate. They poured out of the city to meet the Greeks. There was a great clash of shields and spears. Arrows flew everywhere. Yet, when the first battle ended, no one had won.

The two sides met again to fight the next day. Things turned out the same. They fought for many days, but victory did not come for either side. Days turned into 10 years! That is how long they fought with no winner. Was this some cruel joke of the goddess Athena?

Prince Odysseus was young and strong. He was also very smart. He had an idea. The war was lasting too long. The Greek fighters were weary. They were living out in the open in camps, while the Trojans had shelter inside the wall. The Greeks would have to get inside the walled city. It was the only way they could win the war.

The ancient Greeks were great builders. They built great trade ships and fighting ships. They built wonderful buildings. This gave Odysseus his idea. He told Agamemnon what he had in mind.

Men were sent to a nearby Greek island. They brought back wood. For many days, the men used the wood to build a giant wooden horse. It was almost as tall as the wall around Troy. The horse was hollow inside. It had a space for many men to hide. When it was finished, Odysseus and his men climbed inside it. They were ready to fight when the chance came. The others closed them inside the horse.

The rest of the Greek army boarded the ships and sailed. Were they giving up and going home? No, they were not. They only sailed around the nearest island, out of sight of the Trojan watchmen. They went to hide and wait.

When the Trojans saw the Greek ships sail away, they came outside the wall. They went to have a look at the Greek camps. They wanted to be sure the Greeks were gone. When they arrived where the camps had been, they found a surprise. It was a giant wooden horse! What was it?

The Trojans crowded around the horse. King Priam was there. Inside, the Greek fighters could hear them talking. Some people thought the horse was amazing. Others felt uneasy. Priam was among these. Some people said the horse should be destroyed. They told the king to set it on fire or chop it to pieces. He ordered his men to check the horse to see if it was safe.

As they began to check the horse, a man was dragged before the crowd. He was Greek. He had been left behind when the others departed. King Priam stopped the men from hurting him. He asked the man about the horse.

The man spoke just as Odysseus had ordered, for he was a Greek spy. He told Priam that he had been left behind as punishment for disobeying orders. He said the horse was a gift from the Greeks to Athena. They hoped she would let them sail safely home.

Hearing this, Priam felt they should not destroy the horse. It might make Athena angry. He ordered the people to take the horse inside the wall of Troy.

It was a bumpy ride to the city for the men inside the horse. The Trojans shouted and talked loudly. At one point, they stopped. The horse was too big to fit through the gate. The

gate was removed along with some of the stones around it. Then, the horse was pushed through the wall. The hidden Greeks were inside the city!

The horse was placed near the temple of Athena. A great festival began. The Trojans danced and sang. They ate plenty of food and drank wine. They celebrated their good fortune late into the night. They were grateful to the goddess Athena. The war was over, or so they thought.

One woman did not celebrate. She had a terrible feeling about it all. She knew something bad would happen. Troy was in great danger. She ran through the streets of the city. She cried out to everyone she saw about what she felt. The people did not listen. They thought she was strange. They went on with the celebration.

That night, the Trojans slept deeply. They had enjoyed much food and wine. Inside the horse, the Greek fighters were wide awake. They carefully opened the door in the belly of the horse. Using a rope, they climbed down. They quickly found and did away with the Trojan watchmen at the top of the wall. Then, they lit a single torch. It was a sign to the Greeks hiding behind the island to come back to Troy.

The Greek fighters entered the city where the gate had once been. They attacked suddenly, setting fire to the city. King Priam awakened to the horror. He knew at once what had happened. The Greeks had tricked him.

The city burned for three days. When the fires died, nothing was left. A few of the people escaped, but far more died in the great fire.

Menelaus went back to Sparta. He took Helen home. Agamemnon returned to his kingdom. Things did not go so smoothly for Odysseus. He was lost at sea for 10 more years before he returned home to his wife and son. As for the great kingdom of Troy, it faded with time into dust. The story of its defeat and the wooden horse lives on to this day.

Power in Ancient Greece

Much of the power of ancient Greece came from its military. It had two parts. One was the army. The other was the navy. Both were important to the well-being of Greek city-states like Athens and Sparta. They protected the Greek way of life.

The Army

Each city-state in Greece had its own army. There were rules for who served. The soldiers were trained to fight.

At first, the main part of the army was the cavalry. Its members rode horses. They had to provide their own weapons. That is why most of them came from rich families. Poor soldiers fought on foot. Their weapons were not good. Later, things became better for some of the poor people. They could afford better weapons. Soon, the foot soldiers were the main part of the army. They became known as hoplites.

Hoplites wore uniforms. They differed from state to state. Almost all had helmets. They also had breast jackets. They were first made of bronze. Later, they were made of leather.

Hoplites carried shields. They also had long spears. They used short iron knives. Their legs were covered in bronze. The coverings were called greaves.

The earliest fighters fought alone. Hoplites fought in patterns. One pattern was called a phalanx. It was a long block of men. When the man in the front fell, the man behind him took his place. His own shield and the one on his right protected each man. The last man on the right was always half exposed. The men had to stay in line for the phalanx to work. They had to move together. Music helped them stay in step.

Some men were too poor to fight as hoplites. They could not afford spears or knives. They fought as archers. Some were stone slingers. Others fought with clubs.

One way the army won battles was to lay siege to the enemy's land. They would surround the city. They would burn any crops that grew near it. As its people began to starve, the enemy would give up. Another way they won battles was by using special weapons. One was the catapult. With it, the Greeks could hurl large rocks at the enemy. They used flame-throwers to burn down wooden walls. They used battering rams to knock down walls.

The army played a big part in many battles. One was the Battle of Marathon. The Greeks had a great leader. They also used their mighty hoplite phalanx.

The Navy

Greece has many mountains. They made travel very hard in ancient times. Ships made travel easier. They allowed people to go around the mountains. They also made it possible for the country to have a mighty navy.

Greek navy ships had both oars and sails. They could be used at the same time. In battle, the sails were lowered. They made it harder for the ships to turn. The more rowers a ship had, the faster it went. The first ships had about 50 rowers. They sat in a single row on each side of the ship. The next ships had two rows of oars on each side. These ships were called biremes. The decks of the ships carried archers and other fighters.

Triremes replaced biremes. They had three rows of oars on each side. They were very fast. They had more than 150 rowers. The fronts of the ships were pointed like noses. This allowed the sailors to row fast and ram enemy ships. This would make the enemy ship sink, slow down, or stop. The Greek archers then would shoot arrows at them. They also would go onto the enemy ship and fight hand-to-hand. Sometimes, the triremes would move toward an enemy ship. At the last minute, they would swing away from it. The rowers would pull their oars on board. The trireme would pass close to the enemy ship. As it did, the oars of the other ship were broken. This allowed the Greek sailors to ram the ship and easily go on board. Triremes were the best warships in the world for a long time.

The rowers were great sailors. They were chosen from the poorest Greek men. They understood the sea. They understood ships. In some states, a rich man was chosen to pay for running each ship for a year. These rich men chose the sailors for the ship.

Like the army, the navy was important to ancient Greece. It played a big part in many battles. One was the Battle of Salamis.

Athens and Sparta

Athens and Sparta were powerful city-states in ancient Greece. Each was strong for different reasons. In Athens, life was based on the family. In Sparta, life was based on the military.

Athens was strong because its navy ruled the sea. It was a rich state. The people had money to build many triremes. Their fighters were called to duty only when they were needed.

Athens was the larger of the two city-states. Its people liked art, music, and plays. They found ways to enjoy life. They enjoyed many things from the outside world. People from other lands traded with them. These visitors brought many kinds of food and other items with them.

The men headed families in Athens. Women usually had to stay at home. They made clothes, cooked, and cleaned. Some families had slaves to do work. Boys went to school at age 7. They studied reading, writing, poetry, and music. They also played sports. Girls stayed at home. They learned how to cook and make clothes.

Sparta was known as a great land power. That was because of its army. Its fighters were known for their bravery. They were feared by many other states. Other countries feared them, too. Spartan fighters served all of the time. They lived in army barracks until they were 60. They were well trained. They were always ready for war.

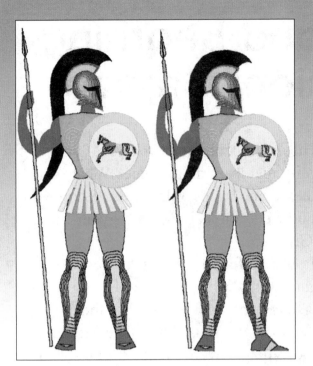

The number of people in Sparta was only half that of Athens. They did not seek pleasure. They chose to face the hard things in life. They did not care for art and music. They did not welcome others from outside their state. They did not care for fancy food or jewelry.

Spartan women had more freedom than those in other city-states. The men lived with the army. The women could come and go as they pleased. Boys left home at 7 years old to learn how to fight. Girls went to school. They learned to read and write. They learned to fight, too. Both boys and girls had harsh training to become strong.

Both states had slaves. Sparta made slaves of its neighbors. Spartan slaves were not trusted. They were watched closely in case they tried to rebel. Slaves in Athens were trusted. They did important things. Some lived easy lives compared with slaves in most states. Many worked as policemen and tutors.

Both Athens and Sparta were ruled in different ways at times. At its height, Athens was a democracy. Both rich and poor people had a say in how they lived. The Assembly was made up of citizens. Citizens were men born in the state. The group made rules about life in Athens. Citizens could vote. Women, foreigners, and slaves could not. Sparta also had an Assembly. It was made of men born in Sparta, but only a few people truly ruled it. This kind of rule was called an oligarchy. In Sparta, only men born there could vote.

Living and Learning in Ancient Greece

What is your way of life? Think about it. Where do you shop? What do your family members do at home? What foods do you eat? Where do they come from? What kind of home do you live in? Where and how do you learn? How is your life like that of the ancient Greeks?

The Greek way of life was different from any other people of the time. They thought about all things in life. Living was more than just surviving. They thought about all of their people. From this, new ways of thinking arose. The people behaved in new ways, too. Villages were planned. Laws were made. People came to know where they fit in. The state of Athens is a good example of how the Greeks lived.

The Agora

In the state of Athens, most of the events took place in the agora. It was a marketplace. Men and servants went there to buy things they needed. Food, spices, perfumes, goods, and slaves could be bought there. The agora  even had bankers. They traded money for the shoppers. Usually only men and servants were seen. The Greeks did not think women belonged there. The men did the shopping for the family. They met their friends there to talk about life, too.

A Woman's Place

Men and women were not treated the same in ancient Greece. A woman's place was in the home. A woman could not vote or take part in politics. She could not own a home or a business. Men in the family ruled her life. She followed the rules of her father, her husband, her brothers, and her sons. She could not work outside the home. Her job was to take care

of the home. Some girls were taught to read and write by their mothers. Later, they could handle the family money.

The rich women could leave home for special festivals. They also could go to women-only dinner parties and some plays. The poorer women could go out more often. They had to do some of the shopping for the home. They were able to see more of life on the outside.

The Greeks liked to have dinner parties. It was the job of women or slaves to prepare the meals. They cooked on grills or over fires. When they baked bread, they used outside ovens. When it was time to eat, women stayed to themselves. They did not eat with the men.

Young women had no say about getting married. A girl's parents decided whom she would marry. Most brides saw their husbands for the first time on the wedding day.

Greek women liked makeup and jewelry. They had special perfume pots. Rich women wore more jewelry than other women. Most free Greek women had long hair. Slaves were most likely to have shorter hair. Married women wore their hair piled high on their heads. They wore a lot of ribbons and decorations. They liked bracelets and earrings. They liked rings, too.

Eat, Drink, and Be Merry

Most of the ancient Greeks were farmers. Rich farmers had servants and slaves who did all of the work on the farms. Poor farmers had to do their own work. The women and children helped. They grew olives and grapes. The people ate olives and used them to make olive oil. They ate grapes and used them to make wine and raisins.

Barley and wheat also were grown. They were used to make hot cereals and bread. Bread was the most important food. Many farms also had crops of beans, onions, and carrots.

The favorite drink was wine. The Greeks always mixed water in their wine. Even though both rich and poor drank wine, the richer people drank more wine. The poorer people drank more water and goats' milk.

Most people ate three meals a day. They ate breakfast, lunch, and dinner. Hot cereal was eaten for breakfast. Lunch was eaten near the middle of the day. It was not a large meal. It was mostly bread and cheese. Dinner was the main meal. It often was made up of fish, vegetables, and cheese. There might be fruit like grapes, figs, or raisins. There also might be nuts like almonds or chestnuts. The Greeks did not have sugar. They used honey to sweeten foods.

Deer meat was eaten at special times. Goat meat was, too. At weddings, these meats were cooked and shared with families and poorer people. Meat also was eaten at festivals.

No Place Like Home

Greek homes were made of bricks. Straw and mud were mixed together and shaped into rectangular bricks. The bricks were dried in the sun. Clay tiles were used on roofs. Shutters covered the windows. They were made of wood. Doors and the upper floors of some houses were, too.

The homes were usually two stories. Most had courtyards in the middle. Stairs from the second story led into the courtyards. The rooms on the first floor also opened to the courtyards. The courtyards usually had wells for water and outdoor ovens to bake bread.

Greeks spent a lot of time outside. The children played in the courtyards while the women worked. They had light from the sun and small lamps that used olive oil. Men lived in one part of the house. Women lived in the other. The andron was the men's part of the home. Parties were held there. Slave boys and girls usually served the guests. The women's part of the house was called the gynaceum. They spent their time spinning and weaving cloth to make clothes. They also made curtains and covers for the couches. Kitchens had fires in the middle for cooking. Bedrooms for the owners and the servants were on the second floors of the houses. Homes of the rich had storerooms to hold food and other items. These homes had workshops for the men, too.

School Days

Not all children went to school in ancient Greece. In Sparta, both boys and girls went to school. Some boys went to school in Athens, but no girls were allowed to go. Boys from rich families sometimes had their own slaves. The slaves were called pedagogues. The slaves went with the boys to school and helped them with homework. The boys went to school until they were 14. Some of the very rich boys could go to school until they were 18.

At 14, they were trained in sports. They learned to wrestle and run. They learned to throw the discus and javelin. They also spent a lot of time talking about math, science, and life. They talked with older men.

Girls were taught much the same as boys in Sparta. This was not true in Athens. There, Greek fathers thought it was best for girls to stay at home. They wanted them to learn how to be wives and mothers. The girls learned to spin and weave cloth for clothes. They learned to run a home and cook. Some mothers taught their daughters enough reading and writing to be in charge of the house.

A student wrote with a piece of metal or bone. It had a sharp point on one end. It was called a stylus. The students wrote on wooden tablets covered with wax. They made marks on the wax with the stylus. They used the end that was not pointed to rub the wax and "erase" the work. The teachers used paper to teach. It was made from the papyrus plant.

THE BIRTH OF DEMOCRACY

Greetings. I'm Salmakis. You can call me Sal. Now, I know what you're thinking. "Who's this little Greek guy, and why is he talking like that?" Well, I'm not your everyday Greek guy, not at all. You don't know me, but I know you. You see, you've been watching your friends check out the sights in my homeland. And, I've been watching you. So, what do you think of the place? It's quite amazing, if I may say so myself. In some ways, it's not so different from where you are. Now, you might look at a guy like me and say to yourself, "What is he talking about?" Well, I'm talking about something your friends the Time Trackers soon will get a peep at. It's called democracy. That's right. Democracy in action—it's a beautiful thing. What is democracy? I thought you might want to know. Listen up.

What Is Democracy?

Rich men and powerful rulers were in charge of ancient
Greece for many years. But, their days were numbered. Things
changed in 508 B.C. One man came to power. He changed
everything. He formed the first democracy. It was a new way
of doing things. It was a kind of government where the people
ruled the people. They were in charge, not kings, not rich men.
It was what we called a direct democracy. That's because every
citizen had a direct say in what went on. They helped make the
laws. They had the power! And, there was more than one way
a guy like me could get his two cents in. I'll use my hometown
of Athens as an example.

The Assembly

Athens had an Assembly. At an Assembly, all citizens met to speak and vote. They discussed how things should work. They talked about laws and rules and more laws and rules. These guys met every 10 days. There was one catch, though. At least 6,000 citizens had to show up. Fewer than that was a waste of time. Nothing could be done. That's where the special police came in. They sometimes went to round up people if more were needed. Imagine that. A guy is just about to sit down to relax with a little cheese and some soft music. But, it's not happening. He gets marked with red and dragged to the meeting. Soon, people began to catch on. Getting them to show up was not such a problem anymore. They learned to do their duty!

Some leaders in Athens gained too much power. Others were just downright unpopular. They had to be put in their places. A vote was held once a year. Each citizen wrote the name of a leader. It was the name of someone he wanted to be rid of. They wrote on pieces of broken pottery. The pottery pieces were called ostrakon. A guy with more than 600 votes had to go. He had to leave Athens for 10 years. This was called ostracism, sort of like the name of the pottery.

The Council

Athens was made up of 10 tribes. Each tribe chose 50 members. They formed a group called the Council. The members were chosen by lottery. They were not elected by votes. This gave each citizen a chance to be part of the Council.

This group of 500 men helped run things in Athens. They planned new laws. They passed their ideas on to the Assembly. They could make some decisions, but the Assembly voted on all the really big ones.

It wasn't all about coming up with a lot of ideas, no indeed. The men served on the Council for one year. At the end of the year, they had to stand before the Assembly. They had to answer for their work. They had to stand up for the rules they made.

The Jury

Have your folks ever served on jury duty? If they have, they can thank us Greeks. You, too, might be called to serve on a jury one day.

Citizens formed juries. Each jury had more than 200 men. Each jury member had ballot tokens. He used them to vote. One token stood for a vote of innocent. The other stood for guilty. Jury members voted by dropping a token into the voting jar. Tokens were then sorted and counted.

A guy in a jam had to speak for himself. There were no lawyers. Speakers were timed when they spoke to the Assembly or the jury. A water clock was used as a timer. When all the water had dripped from the jar, that was it. Time was up.

Military

Citizens had to serve in the military, too. Training to be a soldier was a big part of learning. All men younger than 60 had to go when there was a war. They had to fight in the war.

The leaders were important guys. There were 10. They were elected each year. This was not true for any other group. The ones everyone liked were elected over and over again.

Citizens

Now you've already read about citizens. Let me make sure you're clear about all that. Pay attention. I'm almost finished.

This is the way things worked. All citizens in Athens had to take part in the government. All citizens had to serve some time on the jury. All citizens had to go to war for Athens. All citizens could take a turn on the Council. All citizens could vote on laws. All citizens could give ideas for changing the laws.

Here's the catch. Only free men were citizens in Athens. Women, slaves, and people born somewhere else could not be. This was true even for men born outside Athens. Those guys were called metics. They did not have any rights.

So, you see, Athens was the birthplace of democracy. The idea started right here. Was it perfect? Of course not. But, you have to admit it was a very good idea, if I must say so myself.

Feathers and Foul Play

Narrator:

Demosthenes, the fisherman, is accused of stealing from his neighbor, Homeris, the farmer. Homeris returned several days ago from the fields to find that he was missing a chicken. He is certain, because he is a careful man who counts his chickens every day—even those that have not yet hatched. Demosthenes was seen by one of the other farmers walking away from Homeris's chicken coop with feathers in his hair and mouth. Demosthenes insists that he is innocent— that he only went into the chicken coop to borrow some feathers to fluff his pillow. Did he steal the chicken?

Lead Juror: Homeris of Athens, you say that Demosthenes, the fisherman, stole your chicken. You ask that he be tried and punished for theft. What do you wish to say before the jury?

Homeris: It is a simple matter. On the day of which we speak, I returned from the fields to count my chickens. I count them every day. I know how to count. I was taught to add. I was taught very well. I found that one chicken was gone. My neighbor Philo saw Demosthenes leave my coop covered in feathers earlier in the day. Furthermore, I found balls of gray hair among the feathers in my chicken coop. Look at his head. See how his gray hair is thinning. Demosthenes stole my chicken. As he carried out the dishonest deed, his hair fell out. The gods surely were not pleased. That is all I have to say.

Lead Juror: Philo, what have you to say?

Philo: I saw Demosthenes leave the coop. He carried something in a sack. He was covered in feathers.

Lead Juror: Is that all you have to tell?

Philo: Yes.

Timekeeper: Homeris must speak no more.

Lead Juror: Demosthenes of Athens, it has been said that you stole from your neighbor, Homeris. You were seen leaving his chicken coop on the same day he returned home to find that one of his chickens was gone. How do you wish to answer Homeris?

Demosthenes: I am a simple fisherman. I work hard for a living. I rise early each morning and go down to the sea with my nets. I cast, and I wait. Some days I catch many fish. Other days, I do not fare so well. Still, I work hard every day. When I return home, I am tired.

Not long ago, I returned home to find that all of the fish I hung out to dry had been eaten. My house was turned topsy-turvy. All of the morning's milk had been spilled, and there were scratch marks and fur on my chairs. The yarn in the sewing room had been dragged through the house. I was most disappointed when I went to lie down. That day, my pillow was torn to pieces. I gathered as many of the feathers as I could find so that my wife might repair the pillow. There were not enough.

My wife said to me, "Go and ask Homeris, the farmer, for feathers from his chicken coop." I went to ask at the home of Homeris. No one answered when I called. I only went to take a few feathers from the floor of the coop. I did not take a chicken. I am a simple fisherman. He is my neighbor. I would not steal from a neighbor.

Lead Juror: So, you would not steal from a neighbor. But if Homeris was not your neighbor, what then?

Demosthenes: I am not a thief. I would not steal from any man.

Lead Juror: But you would steal from any woman?

Demosthenes: No, I would not. Homeris may indeed add. But, I must ask. Can he subtract? Perhaps, he ate a chicken or sold it at the agora. And, what of my home? What happened to my fish, my milk, my furnishings, and my pillow? Perhaps, Homeris and I have a common enemy. Or, just a common guest who did not care to seek permission to take what was needed from our homes. I did not steal a chicken. I did not steal anything. You must believe me.

Timekeeper: Demosthenes must speak no more.

Lead Juror: Fellow jurors, you have heard the accusation and listened to arguments on both sides. We must now decide the fate of Demosthenes. If you believe that he stole the chicken, you must say so, and he must be punished. Vote.

The jury casts votes by dropping solid coins into a vase for guilty and hollow for innocent. The vote counter counts the votes and whispers the results to the lead juror.

Lead Juror:

Demosthenes, you have been found innocent of stealing a chicken from the coop of Homeris. You are free to go.

or

Demosthenes, you have been found guilty of stealing a chicken from the coop of Homeris. For your crime, you will pay a fine of 30 drachmas. Go and pay what you owe, and steal no more.

The ancient Greeks worshiped many gods and goddesses. They prayed to them for help. They thought the gods controlled different parts of their lives.

They also had other beliefs about the gods. They thought the gods looked like humans, but they did not die. That was because they had a liquid in their bodies that let them live forever. They lived in the sky. Their home was called Mount Olympus. Their houses were temples. The gods could change shape and fly down to Earth. They were in charge of everything in the world and could do anything they wanted. The Greeks also thought the gods were everywhere giving life to everything in nature. That is why the people took care of the earth. They respected it because of the gods.

The Greeks built temples on Earth. They thought the gods and goddesses could live in them when they visited. The temples showed some of the best work of Greek builders. Temples in the richest states were made of marble and stone. Some had statues of gods or goddesses. They also had carvings.

Some of the most beautiful temples were in Athens. It was a rich state. One temple was the Parthenon. It was built for Athena. She was the goddess of wisdom. Part of the temple still stands today.

Festivals were held for the gods and goddesses. The people left gifts at the temples. They thought the gods would help and protect them if they gave gifts.

Who were the gods and goddesses of Mount Olympus? What were they like? Keep reading to meet them.

In the Beginning . . .

To know the Olympic gods and goddesses, there is much you must understand. It happened before they came to be. I am Gaea. Some call me Mother Earth. The story of the gods and goddesses begins with me.

Long, long ago, I married Uranus, the sky. We were beautiful and happy together. We had many children. They loved me as the mother of all living things. They feared their father. He was mighty. He was very powerful.

The Titans were our first children. They were tall and strong. They were beautiful. Uranus was happy with them. Our other children were not beautiful. Uranus was not happy with them. He wanted only perfect children for the earth.

I began to fear for my children's lives. I was right to fear. One day I discovered a terrible thing. Uranus had sent away the last of our children. Only the Titans were allowed to stay on Earth. They grew. They became more powerful.

I was so sad. I missed my children. I could not forgive Uranus for what he had done. I asked the Titans to fight him. I wanted them to bring back their brothers. Cronus was my youngest son. He was the only Titan brave enough to fight. He fought hard and won. He took his father's place as ruler.

Still, my heart was saddened. Cronus did not set his brothers free. I would have to wait. Cronus would have sons one day. One of them would be stronger than him. Maybe then, my children would be set free.

That is just what happened. Cronus married kind and gentle Rhea. They had five children. But, when each was born, Cronus swallowed him or her whole. He feared that one of them would grow up and take his throne.

Rhea was hurt and sad. A sixth child was born. She knew something had to be done. She sent the baby boy away so that he would be safe. A shepherd cared for the boy. Soon after, Cronus asked to see the child. Rhea gave him a stone wrapped in a blanket. He thought it was the baby. He swallowed it.

The boy was named Zeus. He grew up far away from Cronus. When he was grown and strong, he and his mother tricked Cronus. Zeus was hired to serve meals to Cronus. I helped Zeus and his mother mix a drink for Cronus. It made Cronus spit out the other children. Rhea was happy at last.

A great war began. It lasted 10 years. Zeus and the other children fought with Cronus. Zeus asked for my help. I told him to bring back my lost children. They would help him defeat his father. He did as I said. Zeus and the young gods won with their help.

Finally, I had peace. My children were returned. The wars ended. All was right in the world. Zeus ruled in peace. My children thanked him by making a home for him. It was hidden in the clouds at the top of Mount Olympus. Humans could not reach it. It had a palace and a temple. The gods were safe and could rule together in peace.

The new rulers were dear to my heart. Almost all were family members of Zeus. Each had special powers. Some used their powers for bad deeds. Others used their powers for good. Their stories have been told for years and years. I will share some of them.

Olympic Gods and Goddesses

Zeus was king of the gods. He was stronger than all other gods and goddesses. His symbol was the thunderbolt. He threw it at gods and humans when he wanted to punish them. They feared him. He was wise and respected, too. He cared about Mount Olympus. He cared about Greece. He wanted the country to be strong.

Hera was the wife of Zeus. She was the goddess of marriage and women. She was beautiful and strong. She had good and bad ways.

ZEUS   HERA   POSEIDON   APOLLO

Poseidon was a brother of Zeus. He was the god of the sea. He had a great trident, or a spear with three prongs. He made waves crash on the sea with it. He was sometimes called the "shaker of the Earth." When his trident struck the ground, the Earth cracked and split. He made the first horse, too. It pulled his chariot from the sea up to Mount Olympus.

Apollo and Artemis were twins. Zeus was their father. Apollo was the god of the sun, music, and poetry. He was the god of healing, archery, and prophecy, too. He shot silver arrows from his silver bow. He loved music. He was wise, caring, and thoughtful. He taught humans how to heal themselves. Only Zeus was loved more by the Greek people than he was.

Artemis was the goddess of hunting and young girls. She was a good hunter. She shot silver arrows from a silver bow. She watched over children, mothers, and animals.

Hermes was the god of travelers. He kept travelers safe and gave them good luck. He was the messenger of Zeus. He could fly as fast as the wind. The Greeks told stories about how smart he was. They said Zeus saw his sharp mind and took him to Mount Olympus to make him a god. While still a baby, he left his home one night. He stole Apollo's best cows. He wrapped the hooves of the cows with bark. He tied brooms to their tails and made them walk backward.

ARTEMIS   HERMES   ATHENA   ARES

Apollo was angry when he found out, and he chased Hermes. All the other gods laughed when they saw Apollo chasing a baby. Zeus made Hermes give back the cows. Hermes wanted Apollo to forgive him. He made a lyre from the shell of a tortoise. He gave it to Apollo. Apollo forgave him, and the two became good friends.

Athena was Zeus's favorite daughter. She ruled over wisdom and arts and crafts. She, too, had many stories. One was of her birth. Once, Zeus had a headache. When the pain became greatest, Athena jumped from his head. She was fully dressed for war. But, she did not like war. She wanted peace and fairness. She made many good things. Some were the trumpet, flute, farm tools, and the olive tree. She taught others how to spin, weave, and cook.

Ares ruled over war. He was a son of Zeus and Hera. He was tall and handsome, but not kind. He liked fighting. He caused problems for the gods and humans. As much as Ares liked to fight, he did not handle getting hurt very well. He cried and ran home to Olympus. Zeus often told him to stop crying like a baby. He was not well liked by the other gods and goddesses.

Such are the stories of some of the Olympians. As time passes, people talk of them less. But, they live on in the history of the great country of Greece.

Magnificent Apollo

Keeper of healing, keeper of the sun,
Magnificent Apollo was the one.
Son of Zeus, he painted the sky
As each day rose on the temple at Delphi.
With his purposeful arrows and silver bow,
He slew the mighty Python, a terrible foe.
Master of poetry, master of song,
Few in memory will remain as long.

May the Best Weaver Win

The world of Greek myths was a magical place. It was a place where anything could happen. The impossible was possible. The unbelievable was believable. The senseless made sense.

The ancient Greeks used myths to show how the world worked. Myths made things easier to understand. The myths helped them overcome fears of things in the world. They gave the people peace. They gave them comfort.

In their world, dolphins could speak to humans because they were the first humans. The seasons changed. The Greeks knew the gods were changing where they lived. Lightning flashed when the gods were angry. Beautiful weather meant they were happy.

The myths are the stories that the Greeks told to one another and their children. The characters are gods, goddesses, and humans. Much of ancient Greece has been forgotten. Greek myths live on in the minds of those who have heard or read them.

There once lived a girl named Arachne. She learned to weave. She soon became known as a fine weaver. She thought herself to be the best of all weavers.

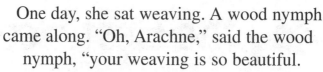

One day, she sat weaving. A wood nymph came along. "Oh, Arachne," said the wood nymph, "your weaving is so beautiful. You must have been taught by Athena herself!"

"Ha!" said Arachne. "I am much better than Athena. She has taught me nothing. I have taught myself everything!"

Athena was the wise goddess. She taught all women how to spin and weave. It was an art. She thought herself to be the best weaver in the world. No god or human was better. News of Arachne's words soon reached her. It made her very angry.

Arachne's attitude scared the wood nymph. She was too daring. The wood nymph said, "It is foolish of you to offend the great goddess Athena so."

Arachne took no heed. She even challenged Athena to a weaving contest. She thought she was sure to win. After all, everyone who saw her work thought she was the best weaver. She would win. Then, she would be the goddess of weaving. She deserved the glory!

Word quickly reached Athena of the girl's conceit. Athena was a peaceful goddess. She set out to try to show the girl the folly of her thinking. She donned the outfit of an old woman. She hobbled to the girl's door. She knocked on it with her cane.

Arachne was surprised to see an old woman at her door. The old woman pointed at her. She said, "You are not wise. Your bragging offends the great goddess Athena. You should be humble. You should not brag about your work. You should bow and ask her forgiveness. Beg her to forgive your conceit. Take back the challenge. You will not like what will happen if you do not."

"You are nothing but a silly old woman," said the girl. "Stop bothering me. I am the greatest weaver. Everyone knows that. Go! Let Athena weave next to me if she thinks she is so great. I do not fear her."

Then, the girl heard a loud voice. "I am here!" it said. Before Arachne's eyes, the old woman became the shining goddess.

Arachne backed away in fear. Her face turned red with shame. Then, she gathered her courage. She said, "Welcome Athena. I do not fear you. Are you not afraid to weave against me?"

Athena looked at Arachne. There was fire in her eyes. The wood nymph had hidden near the cottage. She was terrified. She backed away in fear of what the mighty goddess might do to the girl.

Athena did not say a word. She simply walked into the cottage. The wood nymph came out of hiding. She helped to gather weaving looms and supplies. The looms were set up quickly. The contest began.

Athena and Arachne went
to work. Their hands and fingers
flew back and forth as they skillfully
wove. They used all the beautiful shades
of colors. They wove with purples, pinks,
reds, and blues. They used silver and gold, too.
The wood nymph ran back and forth between the
weavers admiring the beautiful work.

Athena wove a beautiful cloth. It showed the gods and
goddesses. She also showed scenes of what happened when
the gods were displeased with humans. She was trying to warn
the conceited Arachne.

Arachne did not notice. She was busy weaving a beautiful
cloth. Her cloth showed the gods and goddesses, too. But, it
showed their weaknesses. This was one thing she should not
have done.

Athena was outraged when saw the girl's work. It was
perfect. It was better than her own. But, it showed the gods in
a poor light. "How dare this conceited girl disgrace the gods in
such a way," thought Athena. "I will make her pay!" She
slashed the weaving to shreds.

Arachne was very angry. She used one of her strongest
threads to try to hang herself. Athena touched Arachne's
forehead. She made the girl feel ashamed.

Then, she felt sorry for Arachne. "I will allow you to live,"
the goddess said. "But you will forever hang by a thread. You
will be a spider from now on. You will weave your web in the
air forever."

Arachne shrank.
She became a tiny spider.
Her ears and nose fell from her
face. Her lovely weaving fingers
turned into spidery legs. What was
left became a spider body. Within minutes, she was
in the air hanging by the thread. She was spinning the
first spider web on Earth.

When you walk through a yard or garden in the early
morning, watch for Arachne's weavings. She and her
descendants will have left their handiwork on the grasses and
shrubs you pass. They glitter in the morning dew and remind
Earthlings never to dare to compare themselves with the
mighty gods and goddesses.

HERA AND THE TWO BEARS

Callisto was a lovely forest maiden. She was a follower of Artemis. Artemis was the goddess of unmarried girls. They hunted together in the woods.

Zeus, the king of the gods, saw Callisto one day as she hunted. He fell in love with Callisto's beauty. They had a son. They named him Arcus. Callisto and Arcus spent time playing together in the woods.

Hera was not happy when she found out about Callisto and Arcus. She was jealous. She wanted to punish them. She flew down from Mount Olympus and searched the woods. She found them playing a game under a tree.

Callisto was scared when she saw Hera. Everyone knew how mean she was. Hera screamed at Callisto. Callisto begged for forgiveness. Hera did not listen. She did not forgive. She hated Callisto and Arcus.

Hera began to destroy those she hated. Callisto's skin became coarse. Hair grew all over her. Her feet and hands became huge paws. Long sharp claws sprang out of the paws. Terrible sharp teeth replaced her own. When she cried out, it was in a voice that was not her own. It was no longer lovely. It was ragged and deep. Her words became growls. Hera had punished Callisto by turning her into a great bear.

Callisto lost her beauty. She also lost something else. It was even more dear to her. When Hera went away, Callisto turned to Arcus. The boy screamed in fear. He was afraid of the big bear. He did not understand what had happened. He did not know that the bear was his mother.

Wood nymphs heard his screams. They rushed to him. They also found Callisto. She tried to speak. She had to make them understand. It was hopeless. Their eyes and minds were fixed on the large bear towering over a crying child. They quickly carried the boy away to safety. Callisto was left alone.

Time passed. Callisto was forced to hide in the woods. Men sometimes hunted her. Dogs chased her. She ran away from other bears. She did not know how to be a bear. She did know how to hunt. She did not know how to fight like the other bears.

One day, Callisto wandered near a house at the edge of the woods. A child was playing outside the house. It was a young boy. Something stirred in her as she watched him. She dared go closer. Her heart almost burst when she saw that it was her child, Arcus. She wanted to run to him, but she did not dare. She could only watch until he went inside the house.

Callisto stayed as close to the house as she could so that she could watch the child. When he went on walks, she followed along under the cover of the trees. Some nights, she stood at his bedroom window and watched him sleep. Arcus sometimes saw her, but he did not know her. He was afraid of bears. He tried to tell the people who took care of him about her. They did not believe him.

As time went on, Callisto had to move. She could no longer go near the house. There were too many hunters near where Arcus lived. She was forced to go deep into the woods.

Many years passed. One winter night, Callisto dreamed of Arcus. She missed him and wanted to see him. When spring came, she set off in search of him. She found him one day, not far from where Hera's hateful act had changed their lives forever.

Suddenly, she stopped and stood very still. In front of her was a young man. He was a hunter. His arrow was pointed at a small bird in a tree. As soon as she looked upon him, her eyes and her heart told her that the hunter was Arcus. It was her long lost son. She watched with love as her son took aim.

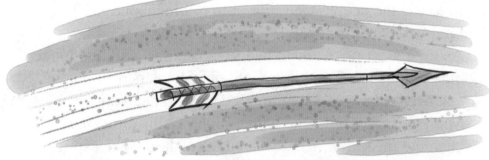

She watched as he let the arrow fly. It missed the bird. The arrow struck another part of the tree. Callisto was glad for this. She had spent years being hunted. She knew the feeling of being hunted and shot at with arrows. She no longer felt as she once had about hunting.

Arcus turned to go, and then he saw her. Fear and panic filled his heart. He raised his bow and arrow to shoot the great bear. Callisto understood, but could not move. She did not want to run from Arcus. She wanted to run to him. But, her arms were now covered in fur. Her gentle hands were big, sharp paws. Her once lovely voice was a terrible growl. She was overcome with sadness and heartache. She waited for death to come.

At that moment, Zeus looked down from Mount Olympus. He saw what was about to happen. In the instant that Arcus let go of the arrow, Zeus streaked down to the woods. He grabbed the bear before the arrow touched her. With the strength that only he had, he flung her into the sky. Then, he snatched Arcus, too. He flung the young man into the sky as well.

As they flew toward the heavens, Callisto and Arcus were changed forever. They were no longer bear and hunter. They became stars. The stars made bear shapes in the night sky. They came to be known as the Great Bear and the Little Bear constellations.

At Mount Olympus, it did not take long for Hera to learn of what Zeus had done. She was not happy that he had saved Callisto and Arcus. She commanded Poseidon, god of the sea, to forbid their drinking from the seawaters as the other stars did. They were never allowed to dip below the horizon for a bath or cool drink. The Great Bear and Little Bear constellations were set in the heavens forever. That is why they are seen throughout the year hanging just above the horizon.

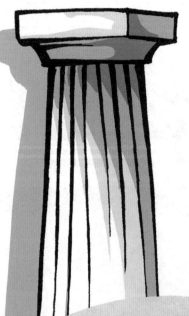

LET PLAYS

Remember me? It's Sal. Do you like going to or watching plays? Do you ever imagine yourself as a great actor? I once did a bit of acting myself. You can do it, too, thanks to the ancient Greeks. You know, it all started with us. This is how it came to be.

THE BEGIN!

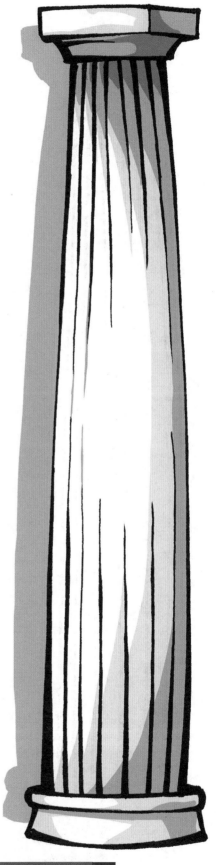

The beginning of plays or theater dates back to a springtime long ago. Where else would it happen but in my very own hometown? It all started in Athens. A festival was held in honor of a Greek god. His name was Dionysus. The people wanted to show their respect. They thought it best to keep the gods happy, if you know what I mean. So, plays were acted out. Writers who wanted to be named "best playwright" wrote them. The plays were held at a large outdoor theater. It seated thousands of people. The actors were almost always men. They wore masks to show the characters they pretended to be.

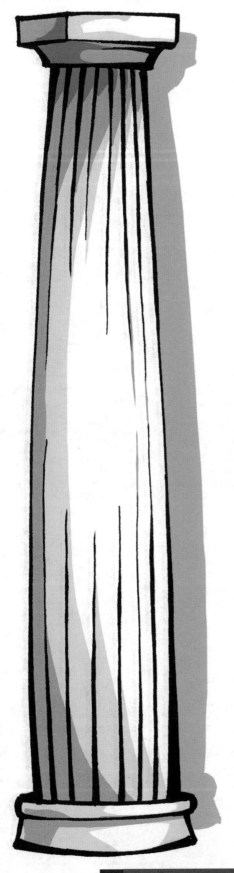

There were two kinds of Greek plays. Comedies were about common people. They usually made fun of Greek leaders. Tragedies were mostly about the gods and goddesses. They told about the troubles of men. Most had unhappy endings.

By the way, you've met one of the top writers—well, sort of. He played host to your friends the Time Trackers. His name was Sophocles. Another was Euripides. They wrote tragedies called Electra. The plays were about King Agamemnon's daughter. You must be wondering where you've heard that name before. The good king fought in the Trojan War. It caused him a lot of trouble later, too. But, that's another story. Euripides wrote in a way that showed how characters felt. Sophocles was first to use decorations. They make up the scenery. He was first to use more than two actors in his plays, too.

Aeschylus wrote tragedies, too. His most famous was a set of three plays. They told of what happened to King Agamemnon after he fought in the Trojan War. I still can't get into that right now, though. Aristophanes won many prizes at the festival. He wrote comedies. He liked poking fun at Greek leaders. One of his plays was called *The Frogs*. Another was called *The Birds*.

Greek theaters had rows of seats. The seats were set up in half circles. The rows farthest from the stage were taller.

Actors stood on a stage. There were rooms at the back of the stage. There, the actors changed costumes. They kept their props there, too.

We found a way to put the gods into the plays. We raised the actors up into the air on cranes. We moved them around the stage. We made them fly like the gods.

Women were not allowed to act in plays. But, they could watch sometimes. Slaves couldn't even do that.

Now and then, the audiences would become rowdy. When they did, they were quickly put back into place. Men with sticks beat those who misbehaved. Sometimes, they chased them from the theater.

Does any of this sound like what you know about plays? Maybe the plays you've seen are very different from those in ancient Greece. But take my word for it. Much of what we started can be seen around the world today.

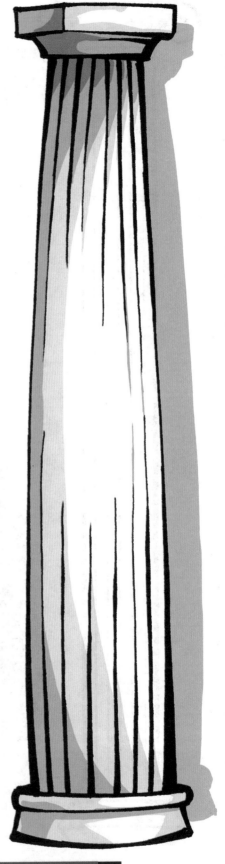

ON BEETLE'S WINGS

Scene: *The cutout of a giant beetle hangs from the ceiling. The background includes drawings of Greek columns or a temple on bulletin board paper. There are clusters of clay pottery and greenery placed throughout the scene. Main actors stand in the middle of the performance area, while the narrator walks to the front center each time he speaks. The chorus is seated to one side of the performance area.*

Narrator: (standing center stage) The war between the two mighty Greek city-states of Athens and Sparta raged. Sparta was wearing Athens down, and food supplies were low. The troublesome Triggy, the vine-grower, decided to take matters into his own hands as usual.

Triggy enters followed by Sickle-Maker and Sword-Maker.

Triggy: Fellow citizens, I tell you that I have had enough! This senseless war must stop. If it does not end soon, it will mean the death of us all. Because no one else will, it is I who must fly up to Zeus, himself, and demand that he put an end to this nonsense.

Sickle-Maker: (holding his nose) Some of us think you should leave matters alone. As long as the war continues, we are happy. Besides, from the smell of things you have other work to do.

Sword-Maker: (holding his nose) Well said, citizen Sickle-Maker.

Triggy: (waves them away) Nonsense. Everyone wishes their vines grew as well as mine. They wish their chickens laid eggs, their horses plowed, and their cows were as full . . .

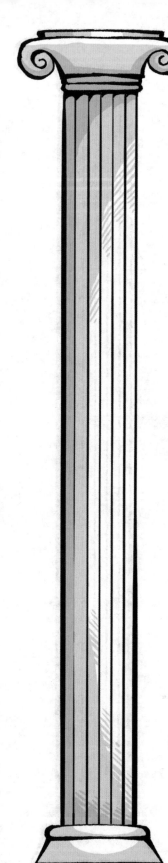

Sickle-Maker: Why, Triggy, that is the problem. Your cows are too full. With as much manure as they give, there should not be a poor vine in all of Athens.

Sword-Maker: Well said, citizen Sickle-Maker.

Triggy: (shaking his finger) Envy, envy, envy. Why, look around. Do you see any manure, or should I say poop?

Sickle-Maker: (looking at Sword-Maker, smiling and shaking his head) He has no idea.

Triggy: (turning to go) I have no more time. I must mount my winged steed and be off to Mount Olympus.

Triggy takes the beetle down from where it hangs and walks out of the room. Sickle-Maker and Sword-Maker leave giggling and shaking their heads.

Narrator: Troublesome Triggy mounted his prized beetle and headed for Mount Olympus to tell Zeus what he must do about the war.

Chorus: Off to Zeus goes Triggy. What will he do? What will he say? Demands? Demands? Demands of mighty Zeus? What will come of this?

Triggy returns to center of performance area with Hermes following holding his nose.

Hermes: You are certainly bold, for such a smelly little mortal. Who are you, and from where did you come?

Triggy: I am the vine-grower, Triggy of Athens. Everyone wishes their vines grew as well as mine. They wish their chickens laid eggs, their horses plowed, and their cows were as full, their pastures as clean, . . .

Hermes: Enough! I'd say your cows are quite full. What is it that you want?

Triggy: I have come on my winged steed to tell Zeus that he must put an end to this silly war between Athens and Sparta. We have all had quite enough.

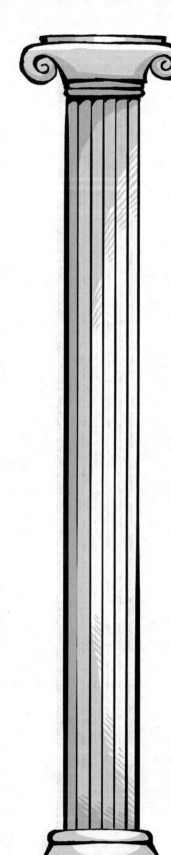

Hermes: (still holding his nose) What winged steed? That thing? (pointing toward the door) That, silly man, is a beetle, and a dung beetle at that!

Triggy: (insulted) Why dung beetle, indeed. I've never heard of such a thing. Now, I must see Zeus. Where is he? (looking around)

Hermes: (smiling) He and most of the other gods and goddesses have gone on vacation until the war is done.

Triggy: Vacation! Don't they understand what is happening to us? Who is in charge while they are away then?

Hermes: That would be War. Come on, stinky Triggy. I'll show you to him.

Triggy and Hermes leave the room.

Narrator: What would War have to say to Triggy? He was a rather dangerous sort with little patience for mere mortals. In fact, he believed that it was his duty to get rid of them all.

Chorus: Poor Triggy, the bold but foolish one, poor Triggy, he knows not what he has done.

Triggy, Hermes, and War enter the performance area.

Triggy: (to War) Just how did you come to be in charge? Where is Peace? I must speak to her now.

War: (smiling) She can't make it. She's sort of tied up now. My, you stink. Hermes said you came on a dung beetle. Why don't you get a horse?

Triggy: I don't need a horse! I need you to bring Peace to me, so I can tell her to stop the war. (yelling) Bring her to me now!

War: (glaring) Silence! Do you dare come here on a stinky bug to order me around? Away with you before I do away with you! Be gone!

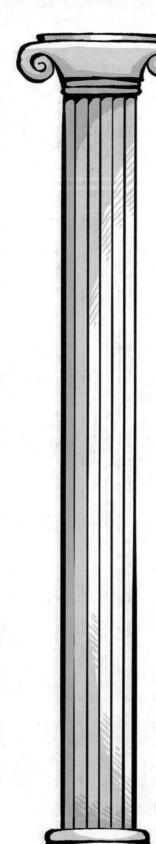

Hermes grabs Triggy's arm and rushes him out of the room. Offstage, he tells Triggy where to find Peace. They go the cave where War is holding her and set her free. She returns to the performance area with them. War is offstage.

Peace: (to Triggy) In return for setting me free, I will do as you ask. Just don't come back up here with any more demands. (rolling her eyes) What is that smell? (sniffing)

Hermes holds up both hands and shakes his head to silence her.

Hermes: The war, he wants it to end.

Peace: Oh, yes, the war.

Peace closes her eyes and raises her hands in the air. Off stage, War screams.

Narrator: Is it over? Did Triggy make the gods end the war?

Chorus: Bold, brave Triggy. Bold, brave Triggy. Bold, brave (one chorus member says) stinky Triggy.

Triggy: Now, that will do nicely. Thank you, and I will be on my way.

Peace: Hold on. Before you go, there's the matter of what Hermes says you call your winged steed. You do know that's a dung beetle, don't you?

Triggy: Oh, in the name of Zeus, what is a dung beetle? I bought that beautiful creature from a foreign salesman at the agora for 100 drachmas. I even have a paper on him.

Hermes: Really? What does it say?

Triggy: Oh, I don't know. I do not have time for such things.

Peace can read minds and knows the secret that Triggy is keeping. She reaches behind her and pulls out a piece of paper with the word "dung" written on it.

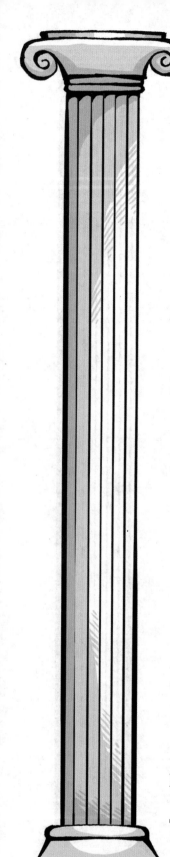

Peace: Is this the paper you were given?

Triggy: (surprised) Why, yes. How did you get it?

Peace: Well, you know we goddesses can do things like that. Anyway, do you know what this says? It says you bought a dung beetle, Triggy.

Triggy: I did no such thing!

Peace: Yes, you did.

Triggy: Did not!

Peace: (places a hand on Triggy's shoulder) It's OK, Triggy. I know your secret. Besides, you say your cows are always full. Well, we know what they do when they're full. And, you say your pastures are clean. Well, what do you think happens to all that . . . stuff? Think about it. That's a mighty big beetle you've got there.

Triggy: (wringing his hands, while Hermes looks on smiling) What do you know about my secret?

Peace: What secret?

Triggy: You know my secret. That's how I bought the beetle. That stinky, stinky beautiful beetle!

Peace: Come on out and say it.

Triggy: I bought a stinky dung beetle because I don't read too well, and I didn't know what I was getting because I couldn't read the paper I was getting. There! I said it.

Hermes: (speaking under his breath to Peace) He could use some help with punctuation, too.

Peace: (leading Triggy out the door, with Hermes following) That's OK, Triggy. Why don't you set your winged steed free and hang around with us for a while. We'll teach you to read. Would you like that?

Hermes: He needs a bath first.

Peace: Hush, Hermes. Come along, Triggy.

Chorus: Hurray for Triggy! Now he will learn to read. (All inhale and exhale in unison.) And now, we can breathe.

Narrator: The End.

THE BEAUTY OF IT ALL

The ancient Greeks worked hard. They fought hard at war. They also enjoyed their lives in a number of ways. They found beauty in music and stories. They found beauty in other forms of art as well.

Music

The ancient Greeks enjoyed music. It was important in their lives. It had many uses. Music played when babies were born. It was played when someone died. There were work songs and love songs. There were battle songs. Music also was played with poetry and theater. What did it sound like?

We may never really know. Most ancient Greek music was never recorded on paper. A few written songs have been found. They are only faded scraps of ancient paper. It is hard to tell what the symbols in the music mean.

What did Greek musical instruments look like? They were pictured on vases and in paintings. One of the main instruments was the lyre. It was strummed like a harp. Another common instrument was the aulos. It was like a wooden flute. Sometimes, people played two at a time. The Greeks played drums, cymbals, and panpipes, too.

The Greeks thought music made people feel, think, and behave in different ways. Some music made men behave calmly. Some music made men behave wildly. The lyre played calm music. The aulos played wild or lively music.

Greek boys studied music at school. Greek thinkers argued about teaching music to boys. Some believed that all boys should learn music. Others did not. People still argue about the matter today.

Spoken Words

Poetry often was heard with music in ancient Greece. It was performed mostly in public. Some men made their livings by speaking poetry. They spoke at parties or festivals. They could recite very long poems.

Homer was a great poet. He wrote very long poems. They were called epics. The poems told stories about gods and heroes. One told about the Trojan War. The Greeks liked it because they had won the war. Another told of one man's long trip home after the war. People still read the poems today.

It was hard for women to become poets in ancient Greece. One did. She became very famous. Her name was Sappho. She wrote many poems called lyric poems. The poems were spoken while music was played on a lyre.

Stories were a part of everyday life in ancient Greece. Some were fables. Others were myths. The men who told them were called bards. They told the stories from memory. Crowds gathered to hear them.

Art

The Greeks made beautiful works of art. One type was pottery. They shaped bowls, vases, and cups from clay. They painted pictures on them with red or black paint. The pictures were just basic shapes at first. Later, the pictures showed scenes from the lives of the people.

The walls of many Greek buildings were painted with pictures. The bright colors have faded over time. Artists were able to restore some of them.

The Greeks were great sculptors. They made many beautiful carvings. Some were statues of gods or goddesses. Others were parts of buildings.

Great Greeks

History books tell many facts about early Greeks. One is that they were great thinkers. They are considered among the greatest thinkers in the world. We call them philosophers.

Socrates, Plato, and Aristotle were three famous philosophers. They asked many questions. They were some of the best students in Greece. Socrates asked and answered questions about how people behaved. He taught about truth and courage. He taught about good and evil. Plato learned from Socrates. He used what he learned to think of other ideas. He thought about how the Greek states should be ruled. Aristotle learned from Plato. He also studied science and math. He taught others. We still use the ideas of these and other Greek thinkers.

Many Greek thinkers were also astronomers. They studied stars. Their ideas helped people to travel at night. The ancient Greeks used star maps instead of road maps. The Greek navy used the stars to find their way at sea. The star patterns were the only maps they had. Greeks traveling on land used the patterns to help them find their way home at night. Some of the star patterns were given names that we use today.

Aesop's Fables:
Lessons for Life

Fables by Aesop are among the most widely known gifts of the ancient Greeks. These stories have been told and read all over the world. People everywhere have learned many valuable lessons from them.

Chapter 1: The Lion and the Mouse

A lion was tired from hunting one day. "That was quite a feast," he said. "I will rest now." He stopped and lay down under a tree for a nap.

A playful mouse lived near the tree. He peeped out of his mouse hole at the great lion. "Why, it is the King of Beasts himself," remarked the tiny animal. "I wonder what brings him here. Whatever the reason, I think I shall have a bit of fun with him."

The lion had begun to snore. "He sleeps deeply," thought the mouse. He quickly darted out of his hole. He ran close to the lion. His heart pumped heavily as he brushed one of its long whiskers. The lion did not move.

"What fun I shall have with the great king," the mouse laughed. "I can tease as I please, and he will never know I am here." He began to run back and forth brushing against the lion's whiskers as he went. It was such fun. But, soon he tired of this game. He wanted to go further.

He darted onto the lion's nose! Suddenly, two great eyes opened in front of him. The mouse froze in terror. The lion had awakened. Then, all was dark. It was as if a great blanket had been thrown over him. But, he knew it was no blanket. It was the lion's paw! He had been caught.

The mouse began to plead with the lion. "Oh, King of Beasts," he cried, "please spare my life. If you will, I promise to repay you some day."

The lion roared with laughter. It was his turn to have a bit of fun with the mouse. "Silly mouse, you dared to tease the King of Beasts. Tell me why I should spare you. You know who I am."

"Oh, I know very well who you are, and I am very sorry. If you will only let me go, I promise to come if ever you should need me." The mouse trembled with fear.

The lion chuckled. "You are quite the funny mouse," he said. "What might you possibly do for one so great as I? I am king, after all. What can befall me that I might have to cry out for you? I'll just eat you right now." He lifted the tiny mouse into the air. He opened his jaws wide.

The mouse let out a tiny scream. "Oh, no," he begged. "You must not eat me. I was foolish. I will never ever tease you again. And, I will keep my word. You will see."

"Is that so?" asked the lion. "Do tell me. What will you save me from, things that go bump in the night?" Tiny tears began to fall from the mouse's eyes. The lion kept up his teasing. "Oh, I know. When I am too tired to hunt, you will bring down my prey and drag it to me so that I might feed. Is that it, silly mouse?"

The poor little animal only trembled more, and the lion began to smile. The thought that he might need a mouse was an amusing one, but it was also pure foolishness. He yawned and let the tiny animal go. To his surprise, the mouse did not run away.

He stood with tear-stained eyes and looked up at the lion. "I will not forget this, great lion. If you ever need me, I will come to you. You will see."

The lion barely heard a word the mouse said. He had drifted off to sleep again. The mouse knew it was best to leave well enough alone. He scurried away. He was glad to be alive.

One day soon after, the lion was out hunting for food. It had been an unlucky hunt. He had come close a few times, but he had not made a catch. His luck was soon to worsen.

He went deeper into the woods. It was very quiet. "This is not natural," thought the lion.

Suddenly, something grabbed him. It lifted him from the ground. The lion tried to strike out with his great paws. He was unable to move them. Whatever held him was not letting go.

The lion became angry. He let out a terrible roar. Birds flew from the tree branches. The lion looked up and saw ropes. Then, he began to understand. "Man!" he thought. "I have been captured in one of his horrible nets. How is this possible? I am the King of Beasts!" Even as he thought these things, the lion remembered stories from when he was a cub. They were stories of Man and his great power. Lion remembered and began to be afraid. He let out another roar. This roar was different from the first. It carried with it the fear the mighty animal felt as it dangled helplessly in the air.

Some distance away, a pair of tiny ears heard the roar. They recognized it at once. Tiny feet raced out of a hole. They hurried not away from the sound of the roar, but to it. It was the mouse. He knew the lion was in trouble. Now, he would keep his promise.

When he found the lion, the mouse scurried up the tree and began to nibble at the ropes. In no time, he had chewed the net loose from the limb. On the ground, he chewed again. This time, the lion was able to tear his way out of the net. Seeing the lion free, the mouse turned to run away. He did not want to take any chances.

"Stop, little mouse," called the lion. "Do not fear. I will not harm you."

The mouse turned to face the lion. "You promised to come when I called if I spared your life. You have kept your promise. I owe you my life." As he spoke these last words, the lion bowed low in honor to the little mouse.

Chapter 2: Turtle and Hare

Each day, Turtle poked along in the forest. Now and then, the other animals stopped and teased him about being so slow. "You're the slowest animal in the forest," they said. Turtle did not care. Instead, he came and went as he pleased.

One day, Hare said loudly, "I am the fastest animal around these parts. I have raced many and won. No one runs like I do. I am the fastest runner ever." Turtle went on slowly, taking his time.

Owl had been watching. "One day Hare will bite off more than he can chew," he said.

Turtle stopped. He liked Owl. Owl was wise and kind. He did not tease Turtle. "What do you mean?" asked Turtle.

"You will see," Owl replied. "You will see."

Turtle went on his way. As he drew near his home, he came upon old Deer. "Do not give too much thought to Hare's boasting," he said to Turtle. "His mouth has always run faster than his feet. He is all talk." Turtle thanked Deer for his wise words and went home.

A few days later, Turtle went for a swim. It took a while to get to the pond, but he finally made it. It was a beautiful day. "Nothing can spoil such a day," Turtle thought to himself. He should have known better.

As soon as he started on his way home, he came upon Hare. Hare stood in the middle of a clearing with Fox and some of the other forest animals. He was talking their ears off. As soon as he saw Turtle, he began to tease him. But, it was Turtle who would have the last word that day. He was fed up with Hare's teasing. He would put a stop to it one way or another.

Turtle stood as tall as his short legs would let him. He stretched his neck to look up at Hare. "I've had it with your boasting, Hare. I will race you—and I will win."

The other animals fell silent. What was Turtle thinking? Surely he did not mean to race Hare! Hare was shocked. For a moment, he did not know what to say. Then, he said, "We'll start with 500 paces between us in a race, Turtle. You can be ahead of me. The winner will be the best racer around here." Then, he added, "That is, I still will be the best racer around here."

"You are quite a joker, but it will be as you wish," said Turtle. He smiled as he spoke, but it was not a nice smile.

Hare saw the look on Turtle's face. He did not know what to make of this. The little slowpoke really did mean to race him! Without another word, Turtle turned as fast as he could and plodded away.

The next day, Skunk and some of the other animals marked the course. Fox was chosen as the judge. He sprinted off to wait at the finish line. The racers took their places. Then, they were off.

Hare went out quick as a wink. He left a trail of dust behind him. Turtle went creeping as fast as he could. The others were sure he would be no match for the fast Hare. Still, he pushed on.

Soon, Hare stopped for a nap. He was sure he had time. He settled down under a tree and was asleep in no time. Hare dreamed as he slept. He dreamed of dust clouds floating in Turtle's face as he sped off. It was a funny dream at first. He smiled at the sight of Turtle poking past him as he slept. Then, he heard cheering, but it was not part of his dream. He awoke and could not believe his eyes.

Turtle was closing in on the finish line. Hare was gone in a flash. He dug deep and gave the race all he had. Terrible thoughts ran through his mind as he ran. They were memories of how he had teased Turtle. They were thoughts of what the other animals would say if he lost the race.

He did all he could to catch Turtle. But, it was not to be. There was a sudden hush. Turtle's nose inched across the finish line first. Long seconds ticked by as inch after inch of his body followed. At last, the tip of his tail crossed the line. The other animals let out a roar of cheers and clapping.

Turtle had won! He was the best racer around those parts. He had outrun Hare.

Chapter 3: Belling the Cat

In a large house, there lived a community of mice. Life was good for a long time. There was a lot of room. There was plenty to eat. One day it all changed. Someone new came to live in the house. That someone was a cat!

Suddenly, the happy days the mice had enjoyed were gone. Now, each new day was filled with dread. The house was no longer safe. In the minds of the mice, terror waited around every corner. But, the terror was not just in their minds. It was real.

Soon after it arrived, the cat made short work of catching the mice. Their numbers began to fall quickly. Day after day, mice disappeared. They were never seen again.

One evening, a meeting was called. When they came together, the mice saw that their numbers had been cut in half. They could not last much longer with things as they were. Before long, the cat would have them all.

The leader of the meeting stated the problem. Something had to be done about the cat. Then, he put forth the question, "What is to be done about the cat?"

Many ideas were tossed around. At one point, a handsome young mouse stood to speak. He had a snobbish way about him that some in the room did not like. Yet, he commanded their attention.

"This is the problem," he said. "The cat is quiet. He is quick. He attacks us without warning. If only we had a way of knowing where he is at all times. Then, we could stay out of his terrible reach."

Soon the room was in an uproar as mice shouted over one another to be heard. The young mouse that had spoken stood watching. He had a sly grin on his face. It was all so simple. Yet, he would not tell them what they needed to know. Let them ask. Let them see how smart he was. He would simply wait.

A weathered old mouse sat in the corner of the room. He watched all that took place, too. He had lived a long life of near misses. He had learned much in his time. His tangled whiskers twitched as he watched the meeting unfold. Looking at the handsome young mouse, he thought to himself, "You have much to learn. May you live long enough to learn it."

Then, the leader turned to the handsome mouse. "You are young and strong. You are smart. Please, tell us what you think we must do."

This was the moment the young mouse had awaited. It was his time to show the others who he was. He stood up straight and cleared his throat. The other mice waited with hope in their eyes.

He fixed the other mice with a haughty gaze. "Don't you know what you must do? Why, you only need tie a bell around its neck." A bell? The others were puzzled. They waited for him to explain. He took his time. "The bell will jingle every time the cat moves. We can hear it and know where he is before he gets too close and pounces." He raised his front paws as if to pounce like a cat when he said this. The nerves of the other mice were so frazzled, they jumped. He laughed aloud at them. The old mouse watched.

Seeing that the young mouse was only having a bit of fun, the others began to laugh with him. The old mouse watched. His whiskers twitched at the thought of what was happening.

Then, one mouse shouted to him above all the rest. "And what say you, old Stubtail? Have you no wise words for us in this matter?" The old mouse said nothing. He simply blinked. It was time for them to remember who he was. It was not luck that allowed him to live such a long life.

He waited for the group to quiet down. They all turned to him. He spoke in a strong voice that did not match his timeworn looks.

"Young one," said Stubtail to the young mouse, "you are indeed smart, but you still have much to learn. Belling the cat as you say is a good idea. Yet, one problem remains." He paused, then said to the group. "Have none of you thought of it?" No one answered. Then, he asked, "Which one of you will put the bell on the cat?" At this, many of the mice gasped. Old Stubtail was not done with them. He had to make sure they understood the lesson he meant to teach. He said, "It is one thing to speak wonderful words. It is another thing to put them into action." With that he pulled his ancient body up from the corner and went home.

The group had been brought down to earth by the words of the old mouse. But it was only for a moment. As he walked away, they dismissed him and turned to hear from the handsome young mouse. He would know better than old Stubtail what they must do. To their surprise, he was nowhere to be found.

Chapter 4: The Grasshopper and the Ants

There once was a foolish grasshopper. He spent the summer days doing much of nothing. He sat around singing. He often was seen skipping along the meadow as if he had not a care in the world.

This was not good in the eyes of the ants. They spent their days working. Winter was coming. They were getting ready. They dragged bits of food into their anthill. "The grasshopper is letting time get away from him," they said. "Sadder days are ahead. He will not sing when winter comes."

Soon, the days grew colder and wetter. The grasshopper stopped singing and skipping. Winter had come. He was cold and hungry. He did not know what to do. Then, he thought of the ants. "They have food," he said. "They will share."

He hopped to the anthill and tapped on the door. "Please let me in, Ants. I am hungry. Will you give me some food?" he begged.

"What song are you singing now that it is cold?" asked the ants. The poor grasshopper did not answer. He hung his head. Thoughts of the summer days he had spent singing and skipping haunted him. It was painfully clear to him. He should have worked like the ants.

As the grasshopper turned to go, he heard a creaking sound. The door of the anthill opened. A tiny ant came forward with a sack of crumbs. The sack was twice the size of its body. "Take this food, foolish grasshopper. Think of it when warmer days return." It dropped the sack at the grasshopper's feet.

"Thank you," said the grasshopper. "I will remember your kindness and your words when warmer days return." The grasshopper picked up the sack and went to look for a warm, dry place to eat.

Chapter 5: The Boy Who Cried Wolf

Once there was a young shepherd. He was just a boy. Life was the same for him each day. Every morning, he rose with the sun. He took his father's sheep out of the village and up the mountain. He spent the day there watching them graze in the pasture. He was always alone in the pasture with the sheep. He often was bored.

One day, he decided to have a bit of fun. He would play a joke on the villagers. He ran down the mountain into the village. As he ran, he cried, "Wolf! Wolf! A wolf is attacking the sheep. You must come at once!"

The villagers ran from their homes and their fields. They saw the look on the boy's face. They heard his cries. Some of the men took clubs, while others grabbed bows and arrows. They started up the mountain. They were strong men ready to do away with a dangerous animal that threatened the sheep. It was a threat to them, too.

The men reached the mountaintop pasture ahead of the boy. With clubs raised and arrows drawn, they looked for the wolf. It was nowhere to be found. Then, they heard something. The sound was out of place. It was the sound of the boy's laughter. He stood near the top of the mountain laughing as the men searched madly for the wolf.

The boy's father called out to him. "Where is the wolf, my son? Where are the slaughtered sheep? There is no blood. What is the meaning of this?"

The boy was barely able to stop laughing long enough to answer. "Father, don't you see? It was all a joke. There is no wolf. All of the sheep are still here. There is no blood. I fooled you. I fooled you all." The boy began to laugh again.

He laughed until his father scolded him. The man was not at all pleased with the boy. The looks on the faces of the other villagers showed that they, too, were not pleased. The men grumbled as they went back down the mountain to continue working in their homes and fields.

Having enjoyed a good laugh, the boy settled down to continue watching the sheep. A few hours passed, but the day was still young. He had several more hours left to watch them. Boredom soon crept up on him again.

"I wonder," thought the boy, "if I can do it all again. I wonder if I can make them come back. It will be such fun to see the looks on their faces—the looks of wild men."

Without a second thought, the boy ran back down the mountain. He cried out louder than he had before. He had to make them believe that a wolf had come to kill the sheep after all. To his joy and amazement, they did believe him. The men followed him once more with clubs and arrows up the mountain.

Once again, they found no wolf. The sheep grazed as peacefully as they had before. The father was beside himself with anger at the boy. He scolded him more loudly than the first time. It was with tearstained eyes that the boy watched the men go back down the mountain to continue their work.

The young shepherd sat down and began to sob in earnest.

His weeping was soon interrupted by the sound of bleating sheep. Something was wrong! He looked up to see the sheep scatter around the pasture. From where he stood, he could make out a dark shape moving among them. His heart sank. It was a wolf—a real one. It was attacking the sheep.

Just as the boy's mind took hold of what was happening, he realized something even more terrifying. There was more than one dark shape moving among the sheep. There was more than one wolf!

The boy flew down the mountain as fast as his legs could carry him. The look of horror on his face was real this time. He cried out so loud his throat burned.

This time, the villagers looked out from their homes. They looked up from their fields. But, they did not come running. There were no raised clubs or drawn arrows. The boy had lied before. They were sure he was lying again. They went on with their work and ordered the boy to return to his sheep.

Back on the mountaintop, the wolves had their fill of the sheep. They carried away what they did not eat on the spot. When the boy did return, he was horrified. Not a single sheep remained. The wolves had destroyed the flock.

Only when the boy came home without the sheep at the end of the day did the men begin to wonder. They ran to the pasture and saw that wolves had indeed attacked the sheep. The father's anger was softened only by the knowledge that his son had learned a great lesson. One danger of lying is that no one will believe you when you finally tell the truth.

Chapter 6:
The Old Lady Who Was Robbed Blind

There once was a wealthy old woman. She lived in a beautiful old house. It was decorated with fancy paintings. It was furnished with plush chairs and couches. The old woman ate from delicate plates. She drank from goblets of gold and silver. All who saw her house spoke of how wonderful it was. She was warmed by their words. She basked in her own memories of the house. She hadn't much else to go on, for her eyesight was rather poor. She could not clearly see many of the objects others found so beautiful. She saw many things in shades of blurred gray.

The old woman called on a doctor. He promised to cure her. They agreed on a fee. The man was a very fine doctor. He was also dishonest.

He called upon the woman every day as agreed. At the end of each visit, he bandaged her eyes. Next, he wished her a good afternoon. Then, he carried with him something from her house.

The doctor did not know it, but the old woman saw what he was doing. She held her tongue. She thought day after day about how she would deal with his dishonest ways. Soon she had a plan.

Before long, the house was almost empty. The doctor had taken all that he wanted. One day, he told the woman that she was cured. She knew the doctor was lying. He had not cured her. It was time to set things right.

The doctor stood before the woman with his hand outstretched. "I'll take the fee you promised me and then be on my way," he said.

"There will be no fee paid," said the woman. "You have not earned it."

The doctor was shocked at this turn of events. "What do you mean? I have made your eyes well again."

"You have done no such thing," chided the woman. "My eyesight is worse than it has ever been. I will not pay you anything. Leave my house at once."

The doctor was angry, but he did as the woman ordered. He left her house. As he went, he promised to take her before the magistrate to be judged. That was just what the old woman wanted. She knew she would triumph over the doctor.

Soon after, the woman was summoned. She stood before the magistrate. He stated the charge. She had been accused of not paying for the doctor's services. "What do you have to say, woman?" asked the magistrate.

"Magistrate," began the woman, "I would like to believe that I have been cured. But, there is one thing that prevents it."

"Explain," said the magistrate.

The old woman continued. "When the doctor first began to visit me, I still was able to see many things in my house. A number of them were little more than blurred gray shapes. Others I saw quite clearly. Now, I can see almost nothing in my house. My nephew Philemon gave me many beautiful paintings. I liked to look at them from time to time. Now I cannot see them at all. It is as if my eyesight became worse each time the doctor left my home. Surely this would not be true if I were cured."

The magistrate was a wise man. He understood what had happened. The doctor was ordered to return the woman's belongings. He was not allowed to collect his fee. The old woman was triumphant.

Chapter 7: Country Mouse, City Mouse

Country Mouse was a plain, kind little mouse. He lived a simple life under the brush at the foot of a great tree. His was a cozy little home. He had planned and built it himself.

The kitchen held stores of food and drink. There was a tiny table with two chairs. In the bedroom, there were twig hooks for hanging the few pieces of clothing he owned. The bed was a mound of dry grass on a twig frame. His blanket was a swag of moss. His favorite room was the tiny parlor. Some of his happiest times were spent there. It was where he often shared light meals and chatted with friends.

Country Mouse loved his home. It wasn't much, but it was all his own. It was also quite safe. It was well hidden from many of the dangers of the woods.

Country Mouse had a good friend who lived in the city. City Mouse was anything but plain. He dressed in city clothes and shoes. He ate city foods. He lived the city life.

City Mouse's home was a hole in the wall of a great house of humans. He had only one room but it was a nice one. In it, he had a bed of the softest cotton. It was a wonderful bed. City Mouse dressed himself each day in front of a fine mirror. It was a small, shiny bronze tray that he had dragged in from the kitchen. He had several sets of clothes made from the cloth scraps the humans left lying around. He dined out each day on bits of the finest cheese and meats. There were also olives, bread, fruit, and nuts.

Life was good for City Mouse. It was also fast. He had to be quick about all of his business. He spent his days darting here for a nibble, there for a quick chat with other city mice. He was always watchful, always ready to dash. That was life in the city. His was not the slow, dull life that Country Mouse lived.

Country Mouse had not seen his friend City Mouse in a long time. He sent word by the birds that lived among the branches above him inviting his friend for a visit. City Mouse agreed to come.

When he arrived, Country Mouse ushered City Mouse into his little parlor. He gave his friend the best seat in the house. It was a little chair carved from a tree knot. Country Mouse had shaped cushions from the most tender grasses and moss that he could find.

They ate from his best eggshell bowls and drank from his strongest nutshell cups. He served his guest wild peas and berries with dewdrop tea. They finished the meal with nuts dipped in honeysuckle syrup.

Country Mouse was so glad to have City Mouse in his home, he did not notice the way his friend looked at the chair he offered. He did not see the odd twitch of City Mouse's whiskers as he sat down to the simple meal.

Soon after nibbling a few bites, City Mouse said, "My friend, I thank you for your kindness, but I must ask. Are you not bored? This is all very pleasant, but also quite dull. Don't you want to know life in the city?"

Country Mouse had indeed often dreamed of what life must be like outside the woods where he lived. He imagined that his friend lived in the most exciting of worlds. He said, "I have thought of it from time to time, but surely that is not the life for me. I cannot imagine it."

"Stop dreaming," said City Mouse. "Come with me and live the life!" At that, he began to tease his friend with stories about food and fancy parties. At last, he stood and said, "Come home with me. I'll show you the city life. It will be so grand."

This was his chance. Country Mouse would see the city! They left right away.

The world was very different beyond the edge of the woods. The sun beamed down on them from everywhere, it seemed. Country Mouse was awed by the changing landscape as they neared the city. Trees disappeared. In their places stood buildings, the homes of humans and other creatures who lived in the city.

City Mouse took him into one of the buildings. Just inside the door, they paused. City Mouse turned and said, "This is my home. We must go quietly from here."

Quiet in one's own home? Country Mouse was puzzled, but thought it best to say nothing. He followed City Mouse as they tiptoed around first one corner and then another. They came to a rather large crack in the bottom of a wall and went in. "Welcome to my home," said City Mouse proudly. He no longer spoke in the quiet voice.

Country Mouse looked around. He saw the bed, the clothes, and the mirror. "It is very nice," he said. "Are all the rooms as fine as this one?"

"Oh, no," answered City Mouse. "I have no other rooms."

"I had hoped to sit and share a meal with you," said Country Mouse. "Where shall we eat? What shall we eat? I am quite hungry now that we are here."

"Not to worry," City Mouse said. As he spoke, he crept back to the opening in the wall and poked his nose out to sniff the air. "We will enjoy a fine meal very soon. As soon as—oh, yes, very soon." He jumped back suddenly as if surprised by something. He seemed nervous.

"What is it, friend?" wondered Country Mouse. "What is wrong?" He started for the opening to have a look for himself.

City Mouse stopped him. "No, we mustn't go out just now. In a moment, it will be safe."

"But we are in your home," said the puzzled Country Mouse. "What danger can find us here? Let us go and have that meal now, wherever it is."

Then, City Mouse made things clear. In another part of the house was a room filled with the most wonderful foods. There were fancy bits of meat and cheeses. There were breads and delightful cakes. Anything a mouse might want to eat could be found there. It was all there for them to enjoy after they got past one thing. It was a very real danger that lurked outside the wall. It was a cat!

Country Mouse thought it was terrible. "Do you mean to say in order to find food you must risk being killed? Do all mice who live in the city face this risk?"

Before City Mouse could answer, he went on. "I'm afraid this is too much for me. My life in the woods may be boring. It may be dull. But, I am safe there. I do not have to whisper in my own home. I have all the food I need, and I can enjoy it without the risk of being killed while I eat. It was kind of you to invite me here, City Mouse. But, I think that when the danger passes, I'll be on my way back home. I would rather eat simple foods in peace and safety than fancy meats and cheeses with danger always lurking near."

Country Mouse waited near the opening of the wall. When he sniffed the air and found it safe, he quickly thanked City Mouse. Then, he hurried back to the woods as fast as his legs could carry him.

Chapter 8: The Crow and the Pitcher

A crow had flown a long,
long way over the
mountains of Greece.
She was glad to see a
village come into
view. She flew over
a courtyard where
she saw a tall clay
pitcher. She was
excited to think
there might be
water in it. If so,
she would be able
to have a drink.
It had been a long,
hot journey. She
was very thirsty.

The crow flew
down to the courtyard.
She could almost taste
the cool water as she
hurried over to the pitcher.
There was water in it just as she
had hoped, but it was only a small amount in the bottom.

The crow put her beak into the pitcher. She could not reach
the water. It was too low. The pitcher was too deep.

"I must have water to drink," said the crow. "I can go no
farther without it."

Then, the crow began to think of ways to get to the water.
First, she tried to break the pitcher. She flapped her wings
against it. It was no use. She was not strong enough to break it.
Next, she tried to knock it over. She ran and slammed her body
against the pitcher. It did not move. She could not knock it over.

The crow sat down to rest. She was weak with thirst. If she did not get a drink of water soon, things would go badly for her. "I cannot get to the water," she said to herself. "Then, I must make the water come to me. But how shall I do that?"

She sat and thought for a while. What was it that the other birds had said about a human making water rise when he sat down in a large bowl? Could it be that if she put something in the water it might rise? It had nowhere else to go but up.

"That's it," said the crow. "I will make the water rise higher in the pitcher, and then I will have a long cool drink." She went to work finding pebbles. She piled them near the pitcher. When she had a good-sized pile, she dropped one of the pebbles into the pitcher. The water rose! She dropped another. It rose again. The crow dropped pebbles into the vase until the water rose near the top of the pitcher.

She took a sip. The water was especially good after all she had gone through to get it. She drank deeply until she had her fill and went on her way.

Chapter 9: The Dog and the Wolf

One night, a dark figure was slinking through the quiet woods. Its shape was outlined in the light of the Greek moon. It moved on four legs with ears at one end and a full tail at the other. The body was skeletal, almost skin and bones. It was the shape of a starving wolf.

Another shape could be seen not far from the first. It, too, moved on four legs with ears at one end and a tail at the other. The body was different. It was smooth and rounded like the belly of a man used to eating well. It was the shape of a well-fed dog.

The shapes moved silently across the soft floor of the woods. Their scents were carried through the air on the night breeze. They drew near to one another. They stopped, listening and letting their senses tell them if they had come upon friend or foe.

It was the wolf that spoke first. "Who walks there?" he asked.

"It is I, cousin. I live on the farm in the village," said the dog. "I am out enjoying a quiet walk in the woods. How does life go for you?"

At that, the wolf stepped into view. To the dog, he appeared to be in his last days. Hunger had taken a great toll on him. The dog said, "Cousin, you do not appear to be well."

"I am well enough," the wolf replied. "I have seen better days on the hunt, but things will turn around soon enough."

The dog said, "You need never go hungry. Come and live as I do with a family in the village. You can help me protect my master's home. Then, you will have plenty to eat."

It was easy for the wolf to imagine the wonderful foods he might enjoy at the farm. He also would have the constant company of the dog, though he was not sure about the humans. Still, he quickly agreed to go with the dog back to the farm.

They started out at once. The dog led the way as they trotted along. As they went, the wolf noticed the dog's shiny fur and strong build. He also noticed something else. There was a spot on the dog's neck where a good bit of the fur had been rubbed off.

"Cousin, I must ask you. What has happened to your neck?"

"Oh, it is nothing," replied the dog. "That is just the spot where the collar sometimes rubs against my neck. It happens when I pull against the chain."

"What chain?" asked the wolf. "Why do you pull against it?"

"During the day, I am mostly tied up with a chain," the dog explained. "Now and then I forget and start to move until the chain reminds me that I must wait on my master to release me."

"Will I also be chained?" wondered the wolf.

"Sure," answered the dog, "but it will not be so all the time."

The wolf stopped. When the dog noticed, he said, "Come on, cousin. We are almost there. Life will be much better. You'll see."

"I don't think it will," the wolf said. "I thank you for your offer. Yet, I would rather live in freedom with hunger than in chains with food. Farewell, kind cousin."

The wolf bounded away deep into the woods. The dog watched him go. As he watched, the wolf's words were repeated in his mind over and over again—freedom with hunger rather than in chains with food.